AF610445

ISBN 978-1-304-66925-4

NURTURING
YOUR CHILD'S
SOUL
SPIRIT
AND
BODY

CONTENTS

DEDICATION

This book is dedicated to my three beautiful sons – Samuel, Peter, and Emmanuel, and to my wonderful husband, Carmelo, who helps me nurture them.

ACKNOWLEDGMENTS

I want to begin by acknowledging that it is God who has inspired the Scriptures from whence I obtain my principles. It is He who allows all of us to have life. It is He who entrusts these three precious children into our care. It is He who provides the wisdom that we seek.

Secondly, I want to acknowledge my dear husband, Carmelo, who aids me in raising our children. I thank him for presenting to them the proper role that they are to assume when they are men.

I acknowledge my three sons, who are available to me to teach and love every day. They are receiving first hand the examples in parenting that are discussed in this book. I am grateful that Carmelo and I have the blessed opportunity to nurture them.

I also want to thank Carmelo's parents, Castrenze and Rosa Turdo, for having raised him to become such a fine man. Their love and commitment to him have been passed on to the next generation.

I thank my cousins, Joseph Booko, John Booko, and Mina and Alfred Sargis, for having encouraged me to write that which is in my heart. Lord willing, their encouragement will result in multiple blessings on families around the world.

I thank my friends, particularly Mrs. Merle Dorn, for also encouraging me in my daily walk with the Lord, and with my family members.

FOREWARD

After reading Susie Turdo's book on "Nurturing Your Child," I was amazed at the extraordinary insight and honest presentation of her subject.

She writes from her heart and the true experiences she has learned as a devoted wife and mother.

As a Spirit-led believer in Christ, she has made her writings based upon the Scriptures.

This book deserves to be read by every parent and all who have any interest in the way of raising children in a joyful and caring way.

I thank the Lord for Susie, and her husband, Carmelo, and their dear sons Samuel, Peter, and Emmanuel – a family of God.

Rev. John Booko, Th.B., M.A.

PREFACE

Thank you so much, Carmelo, for designing the front cover!

The front cover is drawn in the style of a child's art project, complete with each member of the family, and colored with our children's markers. I hope the effect reminds you of a child's representation of his family.

I would like to explain the various elements depicted on the cover. First, we begin with a solid rock foundation, representing God as our strongest foundation. From that foundation emerges growth, representing how we can grow as Christians, and how all family members benefit from that growth. Next, there are intertwining vines. We chose vines because they are strong and resilient. They are very difficult to break. They are intertwining because Jesus is involved in all aspects of our lives. Jesus is the vine, while we are the branches. You also see three boys and a man and a woman. These figures represent the members of our family, although I must admit that we look quite different from the pictures!

In the background shines the Assyrian flag. The flag is there as a thank you to the Assyrian people for their contributions to Christianity. It is also there because it is a part of the heritage in our home. When I see the Assyrian flag, I think about the meaning of the design. The wavy stripes represent the three major rivers of our homeland. Those rivers are the Tigris, Euphrates, and Zawa. The royal blue stripes represent the Euphrates River. Euphrates stands for a word that translates as "abundance." The red stripes represent the Tigris River. Red stands for courage, glory, and pride. The white stripes between the red and blue stripes represent the Zawa River. White stands for tranquility and peace. Some people believe that the red, white, and blue stripes represent the highways that will take the scattered Assyrians back to their ancestral homeland. The sky blue, four pointed star represents the four corners of the world, emanating from the Cradle of Civilization. Its sky blue color stands for tranquility. At the center of the flag is a golden circle. This golden circle represents the sun. Its flames generate heat and light. They sustain the earth and all of its living things.

We know that many Assyrians have been massacred because of their belief in Jesus Christ. To those of you who are living today, remember that His Heavenly Father called you His handiwork. He is a patient and a just God. Do not forget Who blessed you so much to have permitted you to have such a great inheritance. It is He who is permitting us to have the greatest inheritance of all, eternal life. When I see the golden sun in the center of the flag, it makes me think of the Son, whom we love and worship. The choice of a white background for the cover of the book was made because I believe that all that has been written in Scripture is true, and Scripture is my resource for living. Thus, white represents the purity of God's Word.

Thank you very much for reading this book. I hope that you enjoy it!

INTRODUCTION

This volume is intended to serve as a loving guide to those who plan to have children, and to those who presently have children. Grandparents also have important roles in the raising of children. For the purpose of practical application, I have provided some examples from my home. I am writing from my experiences. The principles that we use come directly from Scripture. Here I have provided some of the results of living in the Word. These examples are intended to bless other families, and they are intended to bless God in return for all of the blessings that He has so generously given to us. If anything that you read in this book blesses your home, to God be the Glory.

In the title, three aspects of the child were chosen. These three aspects were soul, spirit, and body. I listed the soul first. The soul consists of emotion, will, and intellect (mind). The soul reflects the child's natural tendencies and inclinations. It contains the child's personality. Parents can appropriately train and nurture their child when they understand their child's soul. Methods of loving, such as displays of affection, teaching, and disciplining will be much more effective once the parents understand the child's soul.

The second aspect of the child that I mentioned in the title was the spirit. The spirit is God-conscious. The spirit is where the Holy Spirit dwells. To nurture the child's spirit, please teach him to study his Bible and to pray for discernment. Discernment is a spiritual gift. It helps the child to see clearly things that appear to be vague to others, or that appear to be the opposite of what they really are. The soul of the child and the spirit of the child work together as a cohesive unit.

The third aspect of the child that I listed in the title was the body. Nurturing the child's body is also important. With a well-nourished body, the child can have a happier soul, because he understands that his well-being is important enough for you to make the best food choices that you can for him. His soul is also blessed because he feels loved and free. He is free from physical burdens that come with poor health. With a well-nourished body, he can think more clearly. When he can think more clearly, he will perform better in his schoolwork. When he has a well-nourished body, he can enjoy playtime to the maximum capacity. This will allow him to get enough exercise to keep his muscles and his mind strong. With a well-nourished body, he will not be ill frequently; when he is ill, it will be less severe than it would be if he were not properly fed. Eating properly and exercising frequently will nurture and delight not only the child's body, but his soul as well.

Another way to nurture the child's body is to have appropriate physical contact. Children, as well as parents, benefit from hugs and squeezes. Children love to be held and rocked. Babies especially thrive on close, intimate contact with their mothers. One of the most comforting and satisfying ways of loving a baby is holding your face against the little one's. When children's souls, spirits, and bodies are nurtured, they have no craving to get physical love from others. This is an especially effective way to prevent children from being victimized by those who are of malicious intent.

When the soul is understood, it becomes strengthened. When the spirit is addressed, the child is conscious of his Lord. When the body is nourished and exercised, the child is healthier, stronger, and more confident. When the spirit and the soul are fed the holy Word of God, the eternal destiny is clear. God reveals Himself to us through Scripture. Scripture says that if we believe in the Lord Jesus Christ, we shall be saved. Teach your child this basic principle of salvation. Teach him the entirety of the Bible.

We, as well as our children, have all been given one soul, one spirit, and one earthly body by our Creator, the Author of Life. We are to care for each aspect of ourselves, and of our sweet children, with great thought, resulting in detailed action. God is triune. We were all created in the image of God. We all have a soul, a spirit, and a body. The body is the only aspect of the child that is temporary. The soul and spirit are the aspects of the child that are nurtured on earth in preparation for eternal life. All aspects of the child should be nurtured so that they will work together to create a person who is strong, virtuous, and resilient. This same child will grow up to be an even more amazing adult, giving all the glory to God.

CHAPTER 1
UNITY

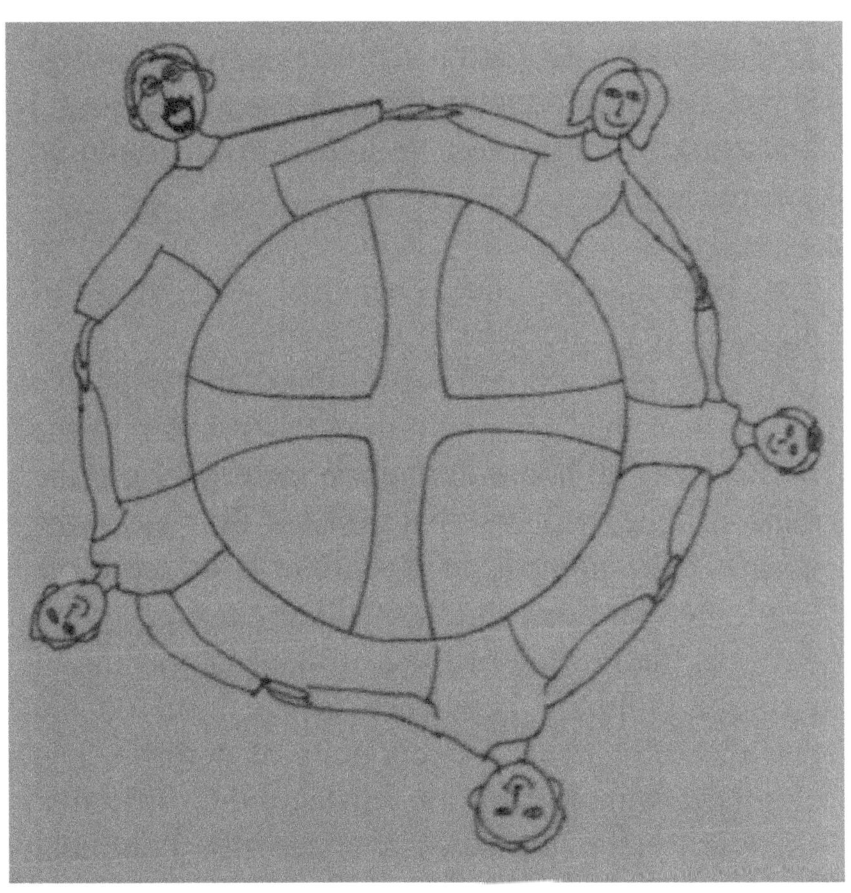

It is important to note that results of the parents' efforts to raise their children properly will vary in degree. Each child has his own personality and time to respond.

An essential element to effectively raising fully developed children is unity between the husband and wife. God is their focus, which brings unity. The by-product of unity is a peaceful, joyful household – a perfect foundation for building secure children.

There are many characteristics in a home that reflect true unity, which I call unity of purpose. If the purpose of the home is to serve the Lord, all permissions, restrictions, and language will reflect that unity of purpose is present. If the purpose of the home is to raise virtuous children, their attitudes will tell that unity of purpose is the norm. If the purpose of the home is to serve the Lord, then virtuous children will be raised.

In the serving of the Lord and the raising of virtuous children, obedience to the Lord on the part of both parents reflects unity of purpose. The children cannot deny or mistake their parents' sincerity. This produces wonderfully confident children.

True unity creates trust between the parents and their children. When parents demonstrate their obedience to God, children pay attention to them, and obey them. The household foundation can only be solid.

There are many ways that parents can demonstrate their obedience to God. Four particular ways come to mind.

The first way that parents can demonstrate their obedience to God is to love thy neighbor. When parents say, “Good morning, Mr. Jones. How are you today?” they are demonstrating courtesy. When parents say, “Excuse me, Mrs. Smith. May I help you with your lawn care?” they are demonstrating compassion in an offer to help. These acts of kindness are real acts of love and respect. The parents stop, notice the neighbors, greet them, and make an offer of assistance. Love is action. To love God is to obey Him.

The second way that parents can demonstrate their obedience to God is to not provoke their children to anger. To aggravate children is cruel and unnecessary. There is no need for parents to lord their authority over their children as a means of oppression.

The third way that parents can demonstrate their obedience to God is to raise their children in the way they should go. “Train up a child in the way he should go, and when he is old he will not depart from it.” Proverbs 22:6. Parents should recognize that it is their job to teach the children about virtues. It is the job of the parents to teach their children about integrity. Begin to teach children about virtues by using the Ten Commandments. This is a great starting point, since all the basic absolutes of human decency are represented. The most effective way to teach children about virtues is to live a virtuous life. Demonstrate the value of absolutes through your own examples.

The fourth way that parents can demonstrate their obedience to God is to love and respect their spouses. God commands men to love their wives. He commands women to respect their husbands. The commandments are not the same, but are equal in value. When children see mercy and gentleness given to their mother by their father, they have viewed the commandment that the husband has been given. When children see honor and obedience to their father’s authority, given by their mother, they have viewed the commandment that the wife has been given. The love and respect that both parents demonstrate to one another provides an excellent example to their children of how they are to behave when they are married.

These four ways that parents can use to demonstrate their obedience to God are all commandments. They are mentioned in various places throughout the Bible. God knows what is best!

Raising virtuous, godly children requires unity between the parents in their goals for each of the family members, obedience to the Lord on the part of the parents, and trust between the parents and children. Trust is earned when the children see that the parents demonstrate their obedience to God. When parents live what they teach, the children find them to be suitable sources of instruction and discipline.

CHAPTER 2
MISSION

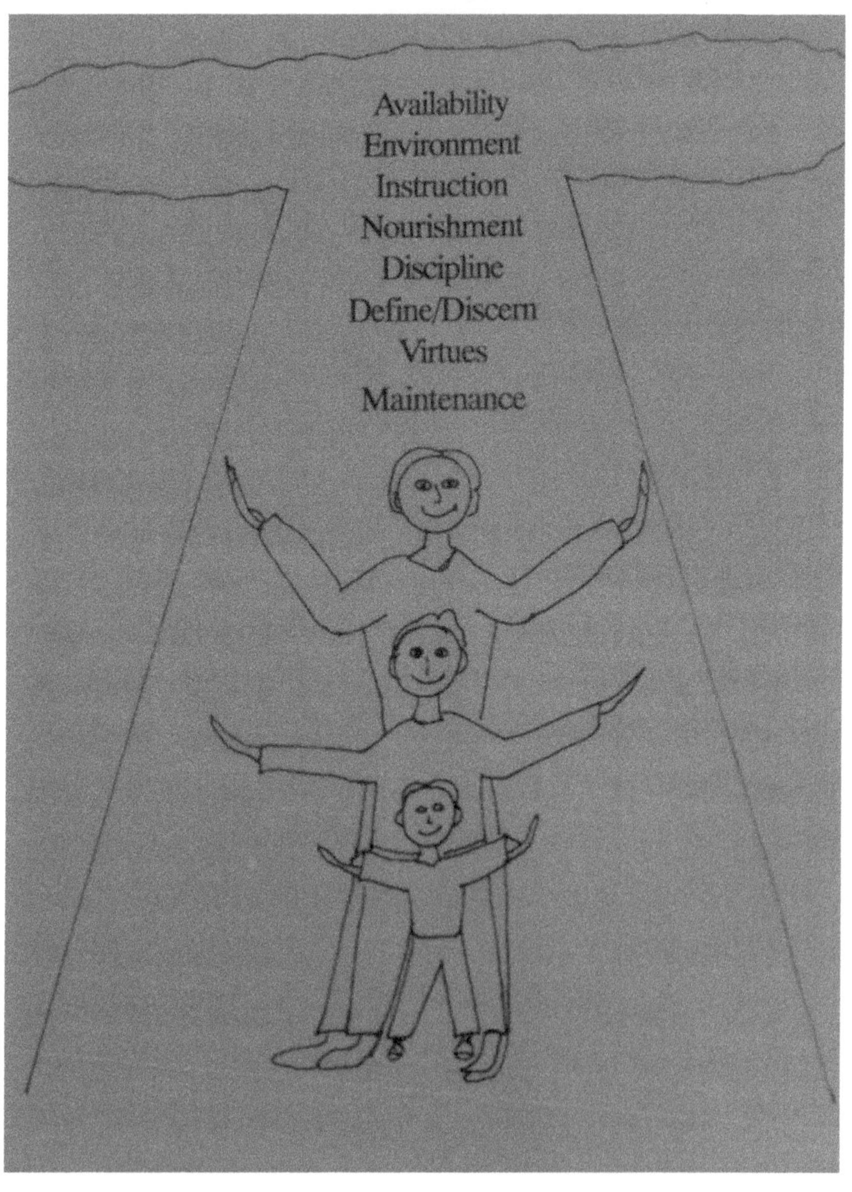

The mission of parents who have unity of purpose is the never-ending process of total child enhancement, or nurturing. The parents assist their child in recognizing and fulfilling the potential that has been given to him by God. All energies of the parents are focused on the mission. When the parents have unity of purpose, they realize that they must do their job right the first time. They cannot re-raise their child.

The first step of the mission is to provide availability of the parents to the child. Both parents should be available to meet the needs of the child. The mother should be available during the child's wakeful hours. When the father is home from work, he should also be available. Availability tells the child that he is important. Be available to hold, instruct, and let go. He matters!

The second step of the mission is providing an environment that is plentiful in love. True love is action. The actions are affection, speech, and care. Affection comes in the forms of hugs, kisses, and smiles. Speech is encouraging and honest. Care is meeting the personal needs of the child, such as cleaning the child and his environment, grooming and dressing him, and cooling him or keeping him warm.

Instruction, nourishment, and discipline will be administered in a home where the child is loved. Instruction occurs in normal daily interactions, through conversation and behavior. Instruction also comes in a more formalized setting, such as a lesson. It is the communication of values from the parents to the child.

Nourishment is both physical and spiritual. The physical nourishment includes the food that the parents choose to prepare for their child, comfort that is readily provided on an unconditional basis, and the exercise that the child performs. The spiritual nourishment is the entire atmosphere in the home, which reflects the Biblical instruction necessary for the success of the mission.

Like all the aforementioned elements that are essential to the second step of the mission, discipline is just as necessary. Discipline has two purposes in this context. One purpose is teaching the child to have self-discipline, or self-control. The other purpose of discipline is the response to an unwanted behavior. If children can exercise self-control, both aspects of discipline have been accomplished. He will discipline himself.

The third step of the mission of total child

enhancement is to teach the child to define and discern. When a child is able to clearly define his universe, and all things in it, and when he is able to discern among those things, he will have learned his most valuable skill for successful living—the ability to think clearly. With this clear, precise thinking, he will know how to learn. He will not be bribed, coerced, duped, tricked, or otherwise treated as though he is ignorant. His environment and his objectives will be clear to him and to those around him. His academics and moral life judgments will be positively affected.

The fourth step of the mission is to teach the child various character traits, and how they relate to him and other subject matter. Uphold Biblical virtues in normal daily interactions, and in the context of an organized lesson. Demonstrate to your child in all ways that character matters.

The fifth step of the mission is maintenance. The parents must always remain focused on the Lord. They must work cohesively whether or not the child is looking. This means that parents should never do anything that discredits the mission of the family. This is the never-ending process of total-child enhancement. It lasts a lifetime.

Availability, love, the teaching of definition and discernment, the teaching of character traits, and maintenance are all essential components to the mission of total-child enhancement. They all nurture the three aspects of the child: the soul, spirit, and body. When parents are available, they are able to love and teach the child, while maintaining the unity necessary to accomplish total-child enhancement.

CHAPTER 3
SOUL FOOD

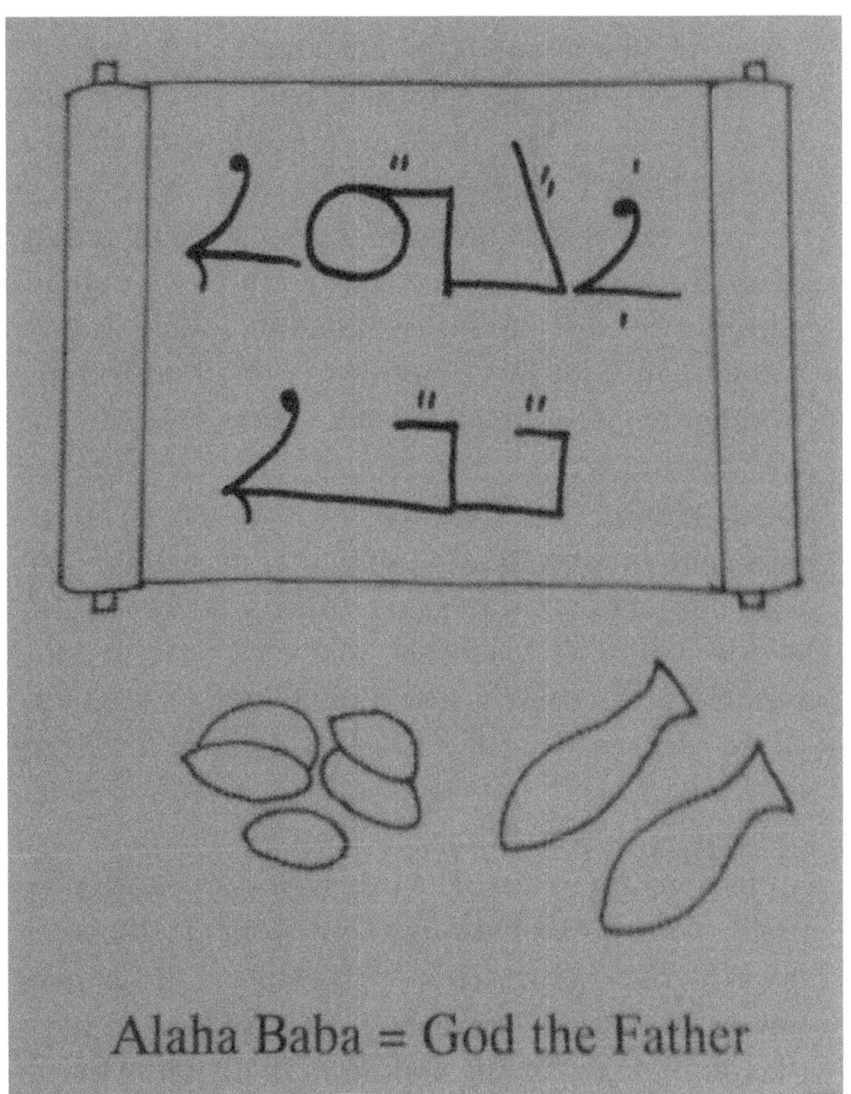

Alaha Baba = God the Father

DISCOVERING AND DEVELOPING YOUR CHILD'S SOUL

As mentioned in the introduction, the soul of a child consists of emotion, will, and intellect. Here are ways that you can nurture your child's soul each day.

Emotions are natural. They can erupt at any time, in any place. A child's emotions can be nurtured by his parents' validation. One way to validate your child's emotions is to embrace him. Another way is to allow him to experience his feelings in private. Sometimes this is appropriate for a painful emotion, or an emotion of rage. When he is able to communicate his feelings, sit with him, and comfort him. Make your best effort to reach him at his heart. Never try to fix the symptoms for him. Encourage him to read his Bible and see what the Lord says about the heart of a child, and how he can reach it to better understand his emotions. When the emotion is a joyful one, be available to share the joy with your child. Remember to not put your feelings as priority over your child's feelings. It is also important for parents to refrain from overindulgence in the emotions with their child.

When that happens, the child gets the message that everything is about you, and that he has no identity of his own. He may then choose to manipulate you by using emotion to get the personal attention that he craves. Be sure that you are available to meet whatever needs your child presents to you regarding his emotions. If he is completely alone when he is experiencing his emotions, he will feel a sense of abandonment. This applies to emotions of pain, as well as emotions of joy. Romans 12:15 says, "Rejoice with those who rejoice, and weep with those who weep."

Will, the second aspect of the soul that I am addressing here, is the freedom of choice that God bestowed upon us when He created us. It is the decisive factor of our soul. The mind carries out what the will decides. Furthermore, God knows what our will shall decide, and what our mind will executc before we know! He knew this before He created us! To nurture your child's will, teach him Scripture, and what it says about wise choices and self-control. In Galatians 5:22-23, self-control is listed as a part of the fruit of the Spirit. That is a reference to the Holy Spirit, meaning God. However, self-control is also in the will of a human, which is a part of the soul.

The mind is the third aspect of the soul that I will address. The mind must be nurtured. If it is not nurtured, it will become idle. When the human mind is idle, Satan may have his way. The child who has not received discernment, and who has not been taught definition, is easy prey for the devil's intentions. The mind needs a daily workout to remain alert and to think clearly. We are told in Scripture to think on that which is lovely, and of good repute. Philippians 4:8.

In these next few paragraphs, I will make references to the child's personality and natural drive.

To understand your child's soul, pay attention to how he functions. Is he victorious when faced with adversity, or is he defeated? Are his shoulders curved and limp, or are they straight and confident? Does he rejoice in the success of others, or does he ridicule them?

If your answers are the positive ones, your only challenge is to keep him living the same way. If your answers are the negative ones, the greatest challenge lies in getting him to understand how precious he is to his Creator. Once he fully comprehends that he was uniquely designed to bring glory to God, his self-esteem will elevate. He will treat others and himself with respect.

Watch your child's tendencies to discover his interests. Does he like to build, read, solve puzzles, or do all of these? When possible, provide the items of his interests, and something different, to which he has given no thought. This will strengthen his confidence by working with things he knows he likes, and then he may feel compelled to try something new. This will enhance the various parts of the brain that deal with different subjects!

Embrace his personality and talents. Show him how to shape them so that they are always glorifying God. After all, He gave them to him!

Be sure to emphasize to your child that his value in God's eyes, and his value in your eyes, is not contingent upon what he accomplishes. His value is based upon the fact that he is a special creation of God's. He is a fine example of God's handiwork and design. He was loved enough to be made flesh, and was sent to you to know and nurture. Our children need to be loved and treasured. They are gifts that have generously been bestowed upon us. They are intended to return to their Maker after they have been held and appreciated here on Earth.

The soul and the spirit of a child are perceptive before he is born, and long before he can articulate what he knows. Conceiving, bearing, and raising children are privileges. They are not rights. Life, at any stage of growth, in any location, and with any circumstances of conception, is sacred. Treat your child as though God is beside you, watching everything you do. Always remember that He is watching you. He is watching all of us. He, in His divine wisdom, has intentionally placed the child that you received into your care. You were chosen to care for that child. Not one of us ever has the right to decide who deserves to live, and who deserves to die. Do not plant the seed of rejection in your child's soul and spirit. Even in the earliest stages of development, he understands in his soul and spirit whether or not he is valuable to you, and whether or not he will be cherished. From the beginning of his life, his soul is crying out to be nurtured and regarded as top priority. The nurturing of your child's soul, spirit, and body is the most rewarding profession, with an excellent, incomparable benefits package.

BLESSING YOUR CHILD'S SOUL WITH MEANINGFUL NAMES

One of the best gifts that we as parents can give to a child is the gift of a great name. A name can provide a standard by which the child can live. A name can establish a great sense of identity. A name can lay the foundation for a heritage that the child can pass on to the next generation.

When our two eldest children were still in God's thoughts, before they were placed in our care, we knew their names. When I was a child I admired and respected my grandfather, Samuel Joseph, immensely. He was a godly man. He loved his family. He worked hard to provide for his wife and children. He had a wonderful sense of humor. He was intelligent and very likeable. When he was preparing to exercise, he would march through his home singing, "Onward Christian Soldiers" in a very thick Assyrian accent. I thought that he had the most beautiful voice in the world! I smiled at him, and watched everything he did. When I was eight years old, I decided that my firstborn son was going to be named Samuel. The name Samuel means, "man of God." My grandfather was a man of God, and I wanted my firstborn son to inherit his precious name. Today, our son Samuel knows the meaning of his name, and he knows about his great-grandfather. Each day, he demonstrates how his soul has been blessed by having received this name. Through his behavior and attitude, he daily lives the meaning of his name. He even has many of the personality characteristics of his great-grandfather!

Samuel's middle name is Carmelo. This is his father's first name, and his father is also a wonderful man of God. He has a strong, humble spirit. He has reverence for our holy God. He is very responsible, and takes loving care of us. He exhibits kindness and respect for me and for my heritage. He takes time each day to spend with his children. He teaches them about science, social studies, music, and primarily about the Bible. He shows his sons how they are expected to behave when they are men, and have a family of their own. The name Carmelo comes from Mt. Carmel. On Mt. Carmel, Elijah confronted the prophets of Baal. The true God revealed Himself by burning up the sacrifice. 1 Kings 18:16-40.

Samuel detests anything unholy. He likes to see his name in the Bible. His comment about his name is that it is a strong, masculine name. Samuel Carmelo Turdo says that when he is a man, he will honor his predecessors by passing on the Christian heritage that has been bestowed upon him. Most of all, he desires to honor God by blessing Him in return for all the blessings that he has received.

Our second son's name is Peter David Turdo. His names also have special meaning. The meaning of the name Peter is, "The rock." We tell Peter that this means that his soul's foundation is solid. He was not built on sinking sand. Jesus said to Peter, "On this rock I will build my church." Matthew 16:18. Any structure that is worth being built, whether it is a physical structure, or a spiritual structure, is built on a rock solid foundation. The intention of building on solid rock is that the foundation will be strong enough to withstand any storm. The foundation and the structure will not tumble into the sea. This is how we are raising our Peter. We teach him that he is not to be broken. With the holy Word of God as his solid rock foundation, the structure of his soul will reflect no damage from weathering. There will only be refining, and additional building. His faith, through the various storms of life, will be refined. His character, through various challenges, will make way for growth and improvement where it is needed.

Peter's middle name of David is the same as his father's middle name. Again, he is sharing a name with his earthly father, who provides the care for our family that our heavenly Father commands him to provide. Carmelo received his middle name of David from his uncle, David Turdo. Peter also enjoys seeing his names in the Bible and hearing his names in sermons. In the Bible, God calls David a man after His own heart. Peter David Turdo says that when he is a man, he will not take his eyes off Jesus. He will stand with the feet of his spirit firmly planted on solid rock, so that no storms of life have a chance to knock him over. Little Peter has such a wonderfully spicy and happy soul, and he is grateful for his names. He is honest and forthright. No one can break him.

Our third son also has two special names. His first name is Emmanuel. Carmelo chose this name as a means of saying "thank you" to God for having blessed our family so bountifully. Emmanuel means, "God with us." Throughout Carmelo's life, and throughout my life, God has made His presence known. He has bestowed great mercy upon us. We are grateful to our holy God, and we want to bless Him in return. When we became aware of the fact that Emmanuel was on his way into our home, Carmelo and I encountered something new in our name selection process. We could not agree on the first name for this sweet baby! So one Sunday, we were sitting in the pew in church, waiting to begin singing. Carmelo looked at me, his eyes filled with tears, and tapped his finger on the church bulletin. He said in a very sweet, soft whisper, "How about this name for our child?" His finger was tapping on the name, "Emmanuel," which was the name of the next song we were going to sing. I said, "Absolutely, yes!" We were so excited to finally know who was on his way into our home!

Emmanuel's middle name is Joseph. Joseph means, "An addition." Emmanuel Joseph Turdo was certainly a welcome addition to our family! I have a cousin named Joseph, who has been a spiritual blessing to our family, and my grandfather Samuel's last name was Joseph. Joseph was the perfect name to pass on to this wonderful boy! His soul is filled with energy and delight. He loves to read Bible stories with us and identify the characters in the stories. He loves to sing about the sweet, holy name of Jesus. Our prayer is that Emmanuel Joseph Turdo will acknowledge and reflect the presence of God throughout his precious life.

One of the many ways that God has blessed our souls through these terrific children has been His perfect timing. All three of them were born on Sundays. They all made their impending arrival known when we were in church, or on our way to church. And, there are exactly twenty-three months between them! Nothing that God allows, or purposely plans, is without meaning or necessity. The soul of any family is blessed when He is the focus of the entire household.

Here are some lessons that can be applied to develop the part of your child's soul that is called the mind. I hope that you will find them to be foundationally sound.

FOUNDATION FOR LEARNING

When you and your spouse first realize that you are being blessed with a child who will receive your nurturing care, begin to teach him immediately. Sing hymns to him, read your Bible out loud, recite the alphabet and letter sounds, and feed him well. Children are not only spiritually aware prior to birth, they are also intellectually receptive. Continue teaching and talking to your child while he is in the womb. When he is born he will recognize your voice, and he will understand what you say.

Please allow me to share some practical examples of what I am writing. When all three of our sons were still in the womb, I read my Bible to them. I prayed for them frequently. I sang hymns to them. I recited the alphabet to them, with all the sound values of each letter. I spelled and sounded out their names to them. After they were born, they were always calmed when I repeated any of the aforementioned examples. As a result of early teaching, they learned to read phonetically between the ages of fifteen and twenty months! They studied with enthusiasm and excitement!

The best time to begin all teaching is while

the child is in the womb. After he is born, begin teaching him to read. Do not teach him to read by sight. Teach him to read by phonetic rules. The child's brain reaches two-thirds of its adult size by the age of three years. From the development time of the brain to age three is the prime time to target his mind. It is far easier to teach him correctly from the beginning than it is to make up for lost time later in development.

When teaching your child, whether you send your child to a school outside the home, or whether you home-educate your child, be sure to teach him the skill of how to learn. Do not teach him disconnected pieces of information. If the child is taught to memorize pieces of information, but has never learned how to learn, he is restricted to those pieces of information. They are valueless. Teaching a child to memorize some facts, having never taught him how to think and learn, restricts his ability to truly learn. A short attention span will develop at a rapid rate, as well as an attitude of disrespect toward study and focus. It is ultimately insulting to a child's potential to teach him pieces of information. He will become repressed in his natural, God-given abilities. A poor attitude and a poor ability to focus will interfere with his real abilities. He can still be productive, but at a greatly reduced rate and capacity. Do not repress your child's will and mind by talking at him, and telling him that he is smart if he remembers the words that you want him to remember.

Weigh all your teachings about virtue and principle against Scripture. Enrich and strengthen his spirit by allowing God to show him and you how your child will best meet his capacity, and cultivate his gifts. Enrich and strengthen his mind by emphasizing the value of thinking before acting. Avoidance of impulsive responses to stimuli will increase long term concentration skills. The spirit and the mind both benefit from thinking skills. The child is less vulnerable to circumstances around him.

LESSONS IN DEFINITION

To define means to clearly identify all characteristics of a subject. Definition is accomplished through analysis. Learning and using the skill of definition organizes the brain. It also allows the child to fully understand whatever he is studying.

The following exercise has two main purposes. First, it will teach the parents how to organize their thoughts when presenting material to their children. Also, it will teach the child to organize his thoughts when learning not only the alphabet, but also any other subject matter. This definition exercise is a lesson in analysis, using basic knowledge as a basis for developing a learning process.

Let's begin by defining all capital and all lowercase letters of the alphabet. We will start by defining how each letter is formed. Diagrams were intentionally left out to train the mind in the skill of taking complex directions.

CAPITAL

1. Capital A begins at the top line, going diagonally down to the left, to the base line. Lift off. Go back to the top point, and then go diagonally down to the right, to the base line. Lift off. These diagonal segments should be slanting at the same degree of approximately 60, from the top line. The two diagonal segments are joined by a horizontal segment, moving left to right, which is halfway between the middle dotted line and the base line. Lift off.

2. Capital B begins with a vertical segment that starts at the top line and goes to the base line. Lift off. Go back to the starting point on the top line, proceed to the right horizontally, curve around down to the dotted line, go in on the dotted line horizontally to the left, until you meet the vertical segment. Go back out horizontally to the right on the same segment, on the dotted line. Curve around down to the base line, and go horizontally to the left, until you meet the end point of the vertical segment. Lift off. The curves of the B should be aligned.

3. Capital C starts under the top line, curves up to the left to the top line, continues curving around through the dotted line, meets the base line, and curves up. Lift off. The beginning and ending points should be aligned with each other. They should also be two-thirds of the distance from the dotted line to the top and base lines.

4. Capital D begins with a vertical segment that starts at the top line and ends at the base line. Lift off. Return to the beginning point on the top line, and make a horizontal segment that moves to the right. Then have the segment curve around down, cutting through the dotted line, and go in to the left on the base line, creating a horizontal segment that meets the endpoint of the vertical segment. Lift off.

5. Capital E begins with a vertical segment that starts at the top line and ends at the base line. Lift off. Go back to the beginning point on the top line and make a horizontal segment that extends to the right of the vertical segment, going across the top line. Lift off. Go to the dotted line where the vertical segment touches. Make another horizontal

segment that moves to the right, going along the dotted line. This segment should be one-half the length of the first horizontal segment. Lift off. The final segment in forming E is another horizontal one. It begins at the bottom point of the vertical segment on the base line and goes to the right, on the base line. It ends when it is aligned with the first horizontal segment. Lift off.

6. Capital F is made the same way as capital E, with the last horizontal segment absent.

7. Capital G is begun as a capital C. A horizontal segment starts halfway between the curved back and the ending point of the C. The segment ends on the ending point of the C.

8. Capital H is made with two vertical segments that begin at the top line and end at the base line. Their distance from each other is equal to half their height. They are joined by one horizontal segment that is on the middle, dotted line. Moving from left

to right forms this horizontal segment.

9. Capital I starts with a vertical segment that begins at the top line and ends at the base line. Lift off. There are two horizontal segments that are added. The first one goes across the top of the vertical segment on the top line. Lift off. The second horizontal segment goes across the bottom of the vertical segment on the base line. Lift off. The lengths of these horizontal segments are one-half the height of the vertical segment.

10. Capital J begins with a vertical segment that starts at the top line and descends almost to the base line. That vertical segment begins its curve right before it touches the base line. Go down from the top line and then curve down to the base line. Curve up from the base line, straightening out when you are past the base line. Stop halfway between the base line and the

dotted line. Lift off. The capital J is topped with a horizontal segment that is the same size as one-half the height of the J. It runs across the top line, moving from left to right.

11. Capital K begins with a vertical segment that starts at the top line and ends at the base line. Lift off. Go back to the top line. Move to the right, using the amount of space that is equal to half the height of the vertical segment. Place your pencil here, and make a diagonal segment that descends to the left and meets the vertical segment at its halfway point. From this same point make another diagonal segment that descends to the right and reaches the base line. Lift off. The point where you lift off should be the same distance from the vertical segment as the top diagonal segment's beginning point.

12. Capital L begins with a vertical segment that begins at the top line

and ends at the base line. Lift off. The base of the L is made with a horizontal segment that begins at the endpoint of the vertical segment on the base line. Its length is equal to one-half the height. It moves from left to right.

13. Capital M begins with a vertical segment that starts at the top line and ends at the base line. The second vertical segment is formed the same way. It is to the right of the first segment. The distance away from it is equal to the height of the segments. Next, make a diagonal segment that begins at the top point of the first segment and proceeds down to the right, to the base line, halfway between the two bottom points of the vertical segments. Lastly, form another diagonal segment that starts at the top of the second vertical segment and moves down to the left, meeting the first diagonal endpoint on the base line.

14. Capital N begins with a vertical segment commencing at the top line and ending at the base line. An identical segment follows. Its distance from the first segment is equal to the height of the segments. The two vertical segments are joined by one diagonal segment. It begins at the top of the first segment and ends at the base of the second segment.

15. Capital O begins at the top line, curves out to the left, cuts through the dotted middle line, curves in to the right to the base line, and proceeds up to the right, cuts through the middle line, and finishes by curving up and in to the left, joining the beginning point at the top.

16. Capital P begins with a vertical segment, top line to base line. The next step is to go to the top beginning point and move horizontally to the right. The last step is to curve around,

out to the right, and then in to the left, finishing with a horizontal segment, moving in to the left on the dotted line. This horizontal segment ends when it reaches the middle of the vertical segment.

17. Capital Q is a capital O, with a tail. The tail begins slightly right of the center of the middle of the O, and halfway between the middle line and the base line. It is a diagonal segment, going down to the right. It ends slightly beneath the base line.

18. Capital R is a capital P with an extra leg. It has a diagonal segment that begins midway on the middle line horizontal segment and proceeds down to the right to the base line. The bottom of this diagonal segment lines up vertically with the outermost part of the curve on the top half of the R.

19. Capital S is formed by beginning beneath the top line, curving up to the

left to the top line, curving around to the right to the middle line, forming a "c" shape, then curving around to the left, touching the base line and curving up, stopping slightly above the base line.

20. Capital T begins with a vertical segment going from the top line to the base line. It is finished with a horizontal segment. The horizontal segment starts on the top line, left of the top of the vertical segment. It proceeds to the right and stops right of the vertical segment. The length of the horizontal segment is equal to half the height of the vertical segment.

21. Capital U begins with a vertical segment starting at the top line. Before it meets the base line, it curves down to the right. When it touches the base line, it moves horizontally to the right, for just a moment. It then proceeds by curving up to the right, and then is totally vertical to the top

line.

22. Capital V is formed with two diagonal segments. One begins at the top line and then finishes by moving down to the right to the base line. The other diagonal segment begins at the right of the first segment and slants down to the left. It meets the endpoint of the first segment on the base line.

23. Capital W is two capital V's put together. The width of each V part is slightly narrower than the capital V.

24. Capital X is formed by two intersecting diagonal segments. The first begins the same way as the first segment in a capital V. The second segment begins to the right of the first, on the top line, and intersects it on the dotted line, going down to the left to the base line.

25. Capital Y is begun as a lowercase v that has its base on the middle line

(see "lowercase v" in the LOWERCASE portion of this lesson). From the middle point, it moves vertically down to the base line.

26. Capital Z begins with a horizontal segment moving from left to right. It moves from the right point, going diagonally down to the left to the base line. It finishes by moving from the base line point horizontally to the right. The top and bottom points line up vertically.

LOWERCASE

1. Lowercase a begins by starting slightly beneath the dotted line.

Curve up to the left, touching the dotted line, and then curve down, touching the base line. Curve up to the right, stopping slightly above the base line. The beginning and the ending points should line up vertically, with the one-half vertical segment drawn through them. What I mean by one-half vertical segment is that it is a segment that begins at the dotted line, and ends at the base line.

2. Lowercase b begins with a vertical segment. It starts at the top line, and ends at the base line. It is completed with a backward lowercase c. The backward c begins on the vertical segment, slightly beneath the dotted line. It curves up to the right, touching the dotted line. It then curves around and down to the base line. It is finished by curving up to the left, stopping slightly above the base line, and on the vertical segment.

3. Lowercase c is formed the same way as a lowercase a, but without the half vertical segment.

4. Lowercase d begins with a lowercase c. It is completed with a vertical segment, on the right side, touching the lowercase c. The vertical segment goes from the top line down to the base line.

5. Lowercase e begins with a lowercase c. It is finished with a horizontal segment, which starts on the outermost left curve, and ends at the top point (the beginning point of the c, which is on the right.)

6. Lowercase f begins slightly beneath the top line. It curves up to the left, touches the top line, and then curves slightly down from the top line, and moves vertically to the base line. It is finished with a horizontal segment on the dotted line, beginning left of the vertical segment, and finishing

right of the segment. The length of the horizontal segment is equal to half the height.

7. Lowercase g begins with a lowercase c. It is completed with a fish hook shape which is attached to the c, that starts at the dotted line, proceeds vertically until it is below the base line, and then curves down to the left, and then up to the left, coming up with a short vertical segment. This ending vertical segment should be lined up with the outermost curve of the lowercase c.

8. Lowercase h begins with a vertical segment moving from the top line to the base line. It is finished with a curve that starts on the l, slightly below the dotted line. This curve goes up to the right to the dotted line, and then curves down to the right. It straightens slightly beneath the dotted line, and moves vertically to the base line.

9. Lowercase i begins with a one-half vertical segment, and ends with a dot. The dot is placed halfway between the top line and the dotted line, directly above the one-half vertical segment.

10. Lowercase j begins with the fish hook shape that appears on the lowercase g. It ends with a dot that is placed above it, in the same manner as the lowercase i.

11. Lowercase k begins with a vertical segment moving from the top line to the base line. The next step is a diagonal segment that begins at the dotted line, moves diagonally down to the left, and ends on the vertical segment, halfway between the dotted line and the base line. The k is finished with another diagonal segment that begins at the halfway point on the first diagonal segment, moves diagonally down to the right,

and ends on the base line. It should vertically line up with the top point, which is the beginning point of the first diagonal segment.

12. Lowercase l is a vertical segment. It starts at the top line, and ends at the base line.

13. Lowercase m starts with a half vertical segment. It is then followed by two curves that are made the same way as the one in lowercase h.

14. Lowercase n is made the same way as lowercase m, but with only one curve.

15. Lowercase o is a circle that begins the same way as a lowercase c, and ends by curving back to the starting point.

16. Lowercase p begins with a vertical segment that starts at the dotted line and ends below the base line,

halfway between the base line and the next line below. It ends with the same backwards lowercase c that is in the lowercase b.

17. Lowercase q begins with a lowercase c. The next step is to form a vertical segment that begins at the dotted line, proceeds down through the beginning and ending points of the c, and goes through the base line. It is attached to the end points of the c. It stops halfway between the base line and the next line. On the right near the bottom of the segment, a hook is added. It resembles a lowercase r.

18. Lowercase r begins with a half vertical segment. It ends with a hook that begins on the segment, just beneath the dotted line, curves up to the right to the dotted line, and then curves down to the right, just beneath the dotted line.

19. Lowercase s begins just beneath the

dotted line, curves up to the left to the dotted line, curves around to the left, around to the right, down to the base line, and finishes by curving up to the left, just above the base line.

20. Lowercase t begins with a vertical segment that starts halfway between the top and dotted lines, and ends at the base line. It is finished by a horizontal segment that begins at the left of the vertical segment and ends at the right of it. The length of the horizontal segment is equal to the top portion of the t.

21. Lowercase u begins at the dotted line, proceeds down vertically until it is just above the base line. It then curves down to the right, until it is just above the base line. It ends with a half vertical segment on this right side of the u, going through the ending point of the curve, and reaching the base line.

22. Lowercase v begins at the dotted line and moves diagonally down to the right, to the base line. It ends by lifting off, going to the dotted line, and moving diagonally down to the left. The two base line points meet at the same point. The distance between the two beginning points is equal to the length of one segment.

23. Lowercase w is made by forming two lowercase v's, side by side. They touch at the beginning point of the second segment of the first v, and the beginning point of the second v.

24. Lowercase x is formed by making a diagonal segment that starts at the dotted line, and moves down to the right, to the base line. Another diagonal segment follows, starting at the dotted line, and moving down to the left, to the base line. These two segments intersect at their midpoints.

25. Lowercase y is formed by making a

diagonal segment that begins at the dotted line, and moves down to the right, to the base line. It is finished by making another diagonal segment. This one begins to the right of the first one, on the dotted line, and moves down to the left until it is halfway between the base line and the next line. The second diagonal segment begins the same distance from the first diagonal segment as the second diagonal segment in the v. This second diagonal segment goes through the endpoint on the base line of the first segment.

26. Lowercase z begins with a horizontal segment that moves to the right on the dotted line. The next step is to make a diagonal segment from this horizontal endpoint at the right. The diagonal segment moves down to the left to the base line. Its endpoint on the base line should vertically line up with the beginning point of the horizontal segment. The z is

completed by forming another horizontal segment. This one is on the base line, and begins at the endpoint of the diagonal segment. It moves to the right, and finishes when it can vertically line up with the first horizontal segment's endpoint.

LETTER SOUNDS AND NON-SOUNDS

In this section of Letter Sounds and Non-sounds, I am allowing extra space to the right of the lists. This space is for you to utilize for taking notes, to add more words that reflect the phonetic lesson of each particular list.

1. A has several sounds. Here are some of the most common examples:

Short A- apple, ant
Dull A- draw, mall
Flat A- atone, umbrella
Long A- ate, staple
Short E A- any, many

2. B has two functions.

Audible B-ball, bring
Silent B- doubt, lamb

3. C has three sounds.

Soft C- city, celery
Hard C- cat, container
CH C- cello

4. D has two sounds.

Soft D- dog, predict
Hard D- baked, talked

5. E has several functions.

Short E- egg, enter
Flat E- the, Nineveh
Long E- equator, equal
Silent E- face, cake
Short I E- business

6. F has two sounds.

Soft F- film, fork
Hard F- of

7. G has several functions.

Soft G- generous, ginger
Hard G- goat, graph
Audible H G- Gila
Silent G- light, gnu

8. H has three functions.

Audible H- harp, help
Silent H- honest, Nineveh
Audible H or Silent H- where, human

9. I has several functions.

Short I- is, intelligent
Long I- ice, island
Long E I- ski, piano
Silent I- business

10. J has four sounds.
Soft G J- jelly, jolt
Audible H J- jalapeno, jaialai
Consonant Y J- Junker, Jung
Audible W J- Juan

11. K has two functions:
Audible K- kite, kettle
Silent K- kneel, knock

12. L has a few functions.
Single audible L- light, curl
Double audible L- bell, millet
Single silent L- balm, could

13. M has two functions.
Audible M- mighty, campus
Silent M- mnemonic, Mnemosyne

14. N has two functions.
Audible N- new, nest

Silent N- kiln (this N can also be audible)

15. O has several sounds.
Short O- ostrich, top
Dull O- orphanage, orthodox
Flat O- potato, tomato
Long O- bone, nose

16. P has two functions.
Audible P- pickle, spoon
Silent P- pseudo, pterodactyl

17. Q sounds like Audible K and Hard C.
Audible Q- queen, Iraq

18. R is audible.
Audible R- rain, project

19. S has three sounds.
Soft S- sticker, dust
Hard S- risen, bus
SH S- sugar, sure

20. T has two functions.
Audible T- table, pet
Silent T- thistle, epistle

21. U has three sounds.
Short U- uncle, drum
Long U- super, student
Short I U- busy, business

22. V is audible. It has the same sound as Hard F.
Audible V- very, vowel

23. W has three functions.
Audible W- walrus, weight
Silent W- knowledge, whose
Audible W or Combined HW- what, where

24. X has three sounds.
Soft X- excellent, exercise
Medium X- executive, exhibit
Hard X- xylophone, xylotomy

25. Y has four sounds.
Consonant Y- yellow, you
Short I Y- physical, hyssop
Long I Y- sky, lyre
Long E Y- baby, jolly

26. Z has two sounds.

Soft Z- zizith, zug
Hard Z- zebra, zipper

Please assist your child in employing the household dictionary. The lists in each of the phonetic lessons should be expanded. Please encourage your child to study the phonetic guides, the parts of speech, language origins, and the definitions of each word.

The most obvious, but equally important skill in letter definition is the ability of your child to recognize all letters in print. This step should precede all others.

The next step in defining letters is to define them by their placement in the alphabet. Here is an example:

A is the first letter. It precedes letter B. B is the second letter. It follows A and precedes C. C is the third letter. It is placed after B and before D.

Use this same method of total analysis, or definition and demonstration of knowledge, with numbers, mathematical symbols (+, -, =, etc.), punctuation marks, and colors. When we first wake up, we look at the clock. There we see numbers. When we say, “Good morning,” to our family members, we are using letters and punctuation marks in speech. When we make our grocery list, we are using letters, numbers, and math symbols. When we are looking at anything, we see color. Everything that we do uses these basic elements. Learning how to define our basic elements (letters, numbers, etc.), as well as learning through Scripture about defining our hearts to better understand our emotions and will, are important steps in nurturing and strengthening your child’s precious soul.

CHAPTER 4
SPIRIT

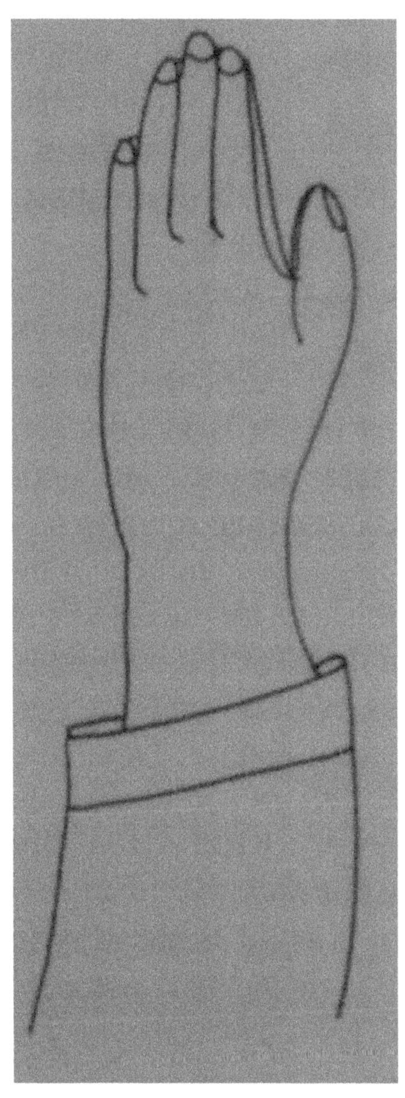

In order to effectively nurture your child's spirit, begin every day with prayer. Pray before each meal. Pray with the child before he studies. Pray with him if he is frightened. Teach him to pray in times of rejoicing. Pray with him before he sleeps. Cover him with prayer when he is with you, and when you are apart from one another. Demonstrate that God always matters, and that He always cares.

When Dad is home, he should lead the family in Bible study. As the head of the household, submissive to the divine authority of God, this is his job. It is healthy for the child to see that spiritual pursuits are appreciated and desired by the masculine members of the family, as well as the feminine members of the family. For a male child, this sets up the role he should follow when he is the head of his own household. For a female child, she will also receive practical insight on how to select a spouse. Her father is the role model for the choosing of her husband. His example shows her what she is to expect when she has a family of her own.

"Train up a child in the way he should go, and when he is old he will not depart from it." Proverbs 22:6. Take this verse very seriously. Let it be your motto each day as you arise from slumber, and begin again the nurturing of your child.

During the early part of the day, sing with your child. Encourage him to enjoy and use beautiful music to offer praises to God, and to sing hymns about His wonderful grace. Elegant, reverent music brings humility and awe to a home. Cheerful, energetic music brings delight into the home. Both reflect a peaceful love for the Lord.

Teach your child what Jesus said, "If you love me, keep my commandments." John 14:8. Teach him that loving Jesus is not a gushy feeling, or an emotional high. It is a disciplined life. It is sincerity. It is his soul's fixation. It is triumphant. It is joy!

The greatest task that parents have in nurturing their child's spirit is the teaching of the plan of salvation. Love your child enough to teach him about the love of God, whom He sent in the person of Jesus. Before Jesus came, He was called Emmanuel. Emmanuel, meaning, "God with us," was sent as a redemption for our sins. When your child has reached the age of accountability and truly understands who he is, who Jesus is, and what eternal life is, encourage him to pray and receive Jesus Christ as his personal savior. If he resists, pray for him and live the example of a Christian life every day. If he accepts Jesus as his savior, what rejoicing for him and the entire family!

When our eldest son Samuel was four years old, he gathered all of us together and declared that he wanted to ask Jesus to be his personal savior. He said that he needed no help in praying. He wanted to use words from his own heart. When he finished praying, there was an amazing illumination surrounding him. The following Sunday he stood before the entire congregation and shared what he had done.

When our second son, Peter, was three years old, he also gathered all of us together and announced that he was ready to pray and ask Jesus to be his personal savior. After he prayed, there was such a beaming smile on his face! He then broke into song singing, "O, How I Love Jesus." The following Sunday, he too stood before the entire congregation and shared with everyone what he had done. He then sang, "Oh, How I Love Jesus!"

Approximately two years before Samuel prayed, and approximately one and one-half years before Peter prayed, they both demonstrated great enthusiasm for reading their Bibles, reading Bible stories, and praying. Before we let them pray and ask for eternal salvation, we questioned them on the character of God, the person of Jesus, who they were, and why they needed to ask Jesus for eternal salvation. We asked them to explain Christianity. This went on for one to two years before we thought that they were truly ready to pray. They always answered the questions correctly. Intellectually, they knew the facts. We also observed their attitudes to be able to properly gauge where they were spiritually. We noticed that they consistently abhorred anything evil. They prayed for one another, and for other family members. They always displayed great discernment on issues that others could not clearly understand, or accurately diagnose. We recognized that both of these boys were aware of their own identity and that of their Creator. Their first answer to questions of others regarding their identity is that they are Christians. Their second response is that of heritage and citizenship. They want to be first identified with Christ, whose heavenly Father created them in the heritage they inherited on earth, and who allowed them to live in this land of freedom.

Our third son, Emmanuel, thoroughly enjoys reading his Bible, reading Bible storybooks, and praying. When he prays, he says, “I love Jesus. I praise Jesus. I obey Jesus. Jesus is holy. Amen.” Those must be sweet words on Jesus’ ears, coming from a two-year old child. Emmanuel also displays reverence toward God, and a respect for things that are sacred. Our prayer is that he too will pray at a young age and ask Jesus to be his personal savior. What a great way to begin life, by starting out walking with the Lord!

LESSONS IN DISCERNMENT

To discern is to see clearly that which is unclear to others. It is also to perceive correctly that which others mistakenly perceive to be acceptable or unacceptable. Discernment comes with wisdom. Wisdom is granted to those who seek it. It can only come from God.

To receive discernment, pray and study your Bible with intensity. If the spiritual gift that God wants you to have is discernment, then he will grant it to you. It has been my experience that those who have the gift of discernment have been people who have prayed and studied their Bibles regularly.

To help your child receive discernment, pray with your child and study the Bible with your child. Allow him to see and hear different situations, non-violent ones only, that are truthful, and also those that are cleverly deceptive. This is a great exercise to gauge and to strengthen discernment. Philosophies that seem reasonable, but have a slight distortion that most people find acceptable, are great teaching tools for lessons in discernment. Philosophies that fit this description are prevalent in schools of all persuasions, sermons, and entertainment. You will have no difficulty in finding examples for your child.

These examples should be judged by the standards of God. If your child is experiencing any ambiguity, or believes in a false philosophy, compare everything to God's word. That is the only source for true wisdom and discernment. The opinions and indulgences of man are vain, but the word of God was written in love. It is flawless. Its truths are timeless.

Discernment is so much more important today than it has ever been. Our society is under attack by the Evil One. Our children suffer because of our ignorance. It is our duty as parents to guard our homes against evil. We cannot afford to fail in our homes. Where we lack enthusiasm, the Evil One will make up for it, with his wicked design. He has no business being anywhere near our precious children. It is much easier for him, with assistance from those who govern our lives, to control a nation whose children are being fed the same nutrient-lacking spiritual milk, than it is to control those who are being fed the convicting meat of Scripture. Not only are there such low spiritual standards, but there are also the same low standards for academic training and expectations.

There is a battle for the soul, spirit, and body of the Christian nation, with so much emphasis being placed on the minds and hearts of our people.

Our first duty is to show our allegiance to our holy God. In our home, we honor our Creator by bestowing upon our children the spiritual gifts that we were given. We give credit where it is due. All that we accomplish is by the grace of God. We consider it to be a grand privilege to have been selected to raise our three boys. In order to display our gratitude to our holy God, we are raising them according to His word. He created them, and He created us. Everyone has a special purpose that He in His divine wisdom has designed.

Secondly, we show honor and respect for our Assyrian predecessors by remembering that they were the first Christians. We are grateful for their repentance at Nineveh. We are grateful that they traveled throughout Asia to bring the good news of Jesus Christ to people of different cultures. We are grateful that our ancestors never compromised their faith in an effort to be accepted in a hostile land. We are grateful that our relatives came to live in the United States of America, so that we would be permitted to freely worship our risen Lord without a daily threat of terror. We honor them by learning their language, Aramaic. We primarily honor Jesus by learning Aramaic, because this was also His language. No nation, whether it is a scattered population, or whether it is contained by borders, has ever been blessed when it took its eyes off Jesus. When Peter took his eyes off Jesus, he began to sink.

Today the Christian nation, identified as a body of believers, is sinking. Christians have a very high divorce rate, and also a high abortion rate. These are such outstanding examples to us of a people being fed milk instead of meat. As parents we must not continue on the same downward, disgraceful, and ultimately destructive trend that has been accepted as popular culture. If we refocus our vision onto the pure white light of Jesus, our homes will be havens for our children, and all family members. We must care about our heritage and not shame it by lacking discernment. We must care about our country and not shame it by exercising a lack of self-control. We must care about our Christian nation, the body of Christ, and not make a mockery of ourselves by using poor judgment and refusing mercy towards our mothers and fathers, sisters and brothers, and children. We must show mercy to our children by training them up in the way they should go. That way is clearly written in the Scriptures. Teach your child discernment so that he is not tricked. We must care about the condition of our hearts as individuals, because Jesus sees how we have restricted His blood flow through our lives. We must care about Jesus, and how we have broken His heart. In all of our homes, we must pledge allegiance to the Lamb. All the rest is a by-product of our hearts' getting right with God. We must have the discernment to proclaim, "As for me and my house, we will serve the Lord." Joshua 24:15.

When you go to sleep after a day of training a child in the way he should go, you will rest assured that he has been blessed by your consideration of what is best for him. Nurturing his soul and his spirit has everlasting rewards.

CHAPTER 5
THE BODY: THE IMPORTANCE OF PHYSICAL NOURISHMENT

Proper diet and exercise are indispensable to the cause of nurturing the child's whole being. Everything that he eats should be highly nutritious. I recommend that, as much as possible, avoid processed foods of any kind, refined foods, and preservatives. These foods damage the immune system, promote low muscle tone, diminish bone density, release toxins into the bloodstream, and selfishly take the place of natural, nutrient-rich foods that could be consumed and enjoyed. Exercise must come after nutritious food has been eaten. Exercise and poor diet do more damage than no exercise and poor diet. Exercising after eating poorly extracts energy and nutrients that arc not there to take, thus making the body overwork.

If anything can be eaten raw, eat it raw. Fruits, vegetables, and herbs are an excellent source of immune system bolstering nutrients, muscle toning nutrients, bone density enhancers, and natural chemicals that increase intelligence. Whole grains, seeds, nuts, beans, lean meats, and dairy products also have these benefits. There is also a nutrient called choline, which is an intelligence stimulator. It is found in eggs and peanuts!

There are a couple of points that I want to make regarding food consumption and the purpose of food. Regarding food consumption, food should be eaten at an easy, slow pace. It should never be eaten in a rush. When food is eaten hurriedly, it is not enjoyed, and it will cause chest and abdominal pain. The second point that I want to make regarding the purpose of food is that food should never be used as a reward for an achievement, and it should never be used as a means of satisfaction. Much of the obesity that children are suffering is due to a warped attitude toward food. Food should be viewed as a source of nourishment to be enjoyed in the company of loved ones. Its purpose is to feed our bodies and minds the nutrients that they need to live well and be most effective. It is a very selfish and ultimately self-destructive behavior pattern to eat for comfort or for reward. We, as the parents of precious children, must love our children enough to not let them abuse their bodies. When we see our children becoming heavy, and when we see them experiencing difficulty behaving in the excitable, energetic way that children should, we have to reverse our methods. It is cruel to let a child's nourishment go unchecked. He will undergo ridicule due to our poor judgment. Before you feed something to your child, ask yourself why you are feeding it to him. Before you feed something to your child, ask yourself why you are feeding it to him. Before you feed something to your child, ask yourself what are the nutritional benefits to your child of that particular food choice.

When the bloodstream is clean, there is less illness and laziness. The mind is clearer. With proper diet and exercise, the child will be more effective in studies and in behavior.

Exercise can be moving around inside the home doing housework, or running, jumping, riding a bicycle, or playing any sport outside. Basketball and tennis are active sports, and are also relatively safe. Playing on swing sets and swimming are great ways to enjoy recreational fun, too!

Exercises that require cardiovascular exertion promote memory enhancement. Eating foods rich in magnesium, such as bananas, do the same. So eat bananas and use your jump rope. They are good for your memory!

Another form of physical nourishment that I mentioned earlier in the Introduction is appropriate physical contact between the parents and the child. Many studies have revealed the various benefits of parent/child physical contact. One benefit is that if the child is given hugs and kisses generously, he has less need to seek physical satisfaction from non-family members. Another benefit of physical contact between parents and their child is a strengthened immune system. When a child is held and comforted, his own stress level is greatly reduced. This allows his body to use its energy in productive, healthy ways. He does not have to make up for what his parents are not doing.

Many of the children who are frequently ill are children who are not top priority to their parents. They do not receive proper nutrition, and they also do not receive unconditional love from their parents. Their parents are usually not caring for them during the day. They are generally under the care of someone else, and are only one in a number of many other children. These other children are also left in the care of someone else, who is other than their own parents. Thus, they suffer many of the same physical, emotional, and social maladies. The parents' unavailability to their children causes these children to become ill more frequently than those whose parents are around them all the time. The unavailability of parents to their children also causes these children to seek physical love from strangers. This makes them highly susceptible to the advances of those who do not have the children's best interests at heart.

A third benefit of appropriate physical contact between parents and their child is the benefit of great enthusiasm for things that are good. Children who are accustomed to receiving hugs and kisses from their parents are usually happier, and are more energetic towards productive pursuits.

Another simple and highly yielding way to have physical contact between parents and their child is the playing of indoor games together. Playing a board game or playing with toys are ways that parents can make themselves available to their child. Most of the time when children ask their parents to play with them, they are seeking companionship and availability. In case they want to hug their parents, or see their parents smile at them and each other, availability, which produces closeness, is necessary.

Playing sports outside or picnicking in the yard or in a park, are other ways that parents can nurture their child physically. Getting fresh air and exercise helps a family to bond in ways that they cannot bond indoors. Fresh air helps everyone stay healthy. Playing sports keeps the body fit and reduces anxiety. Therefore, the body is healthy and relaxed. The mind also benefits from fresh air and exercise. People experience many of their most exciting inspirations when they are outdoors and socializing with those they love.

Another way to nurture your child's body, which will also affect his soul, is making sure that he receives plenty of rest. Rest provides regeneration for his physical strength. The body has a chance to recharge its energy source when he rests without interruption for an ample amount of time. I recommend twelve hours of sleep every night for children two to seven years of age.

Rest affects his soul positively as well, because when the soul rests, it clears and becomes refreshed. Concentration and success are much easier for him when he is not focused on resisting sleep. If possible, provide a quiet environment in the nighttime for your child, and all other family members. Providing quiet when it is time to sleep teaches him that he, and his real needs, are respected. He in turn will be likely to respect others when their time of need arrives.

CHAPTER 6

HOME-BASED EDUCATION

For those of you who are interested in educating your children at home, please allow me to express to you how tremendously rewarding home-based education can be to a family.

I must begin by saying that research into your local laws is imperative to having successful home-based education, or homeschooling. Some states have mandatory registration, which means that you are accountable to your local government officials. In the states with mandatory registration, there may be regulation of the instructional materials that are to be used for teaching your child at home. In the states with mandatory registration, there is usually mandatory testing of your child's achievements for that particular school year. There sometimes is a requirement to produce proof of your child's work and/or your child's grades and his daily schedule. Some states require testing of achievement, proof of work, and submission of grades and daily schedule biannually. Some states make these requirements annually.

In the state of Missouri, where we live, the laws are quite favorable toward home education. We have the freedom to choose any curriculum that we deem appropriate for our children. We do not have to register our children as homeschoolers with any local officials. There is no mandatory testing or reporting of grades or daily schedule. We are required to keep a daily account of class work, with the amount of course hours logged. This record keeping is required because there is the possibility that someone may report you for not having your child enrolled in a public or private school. If anyone inquires about your child's educational style, you have only to say that he is being homeschooled.

The legal reason for keeping records is in case a prosecuting attorney arrives at your home. Someone would have had to claim that there was educational neglect or abuse of some kind to the child. A prosecuting attorney, in the state of Missouri, is the only person who is permitted by law to see your records and to question you, the parent. If home-based education is done properly, there will be no neglect or abuse of any kind. Remember, your whole purpose is to nurture your child's soul, spirit, and body.

Here are some of the rewards that we, as a family of home educators and students, have experienced over the years. The first one that comes to mind is that we have the ability to raise our children in the way they should go, every day. Their spiritual welfare is so incredibly important. Their relationship with their Creator is the purpose of their existence. When the majority of their time is spent solidifying their firm foundation, the time they spend in the world socializing with those who have different beliefs, is unthreatening.

Another reward that we have experienced as a family of home educators and students is the availability that we have to our children. We are around to answer their questions, hold them when they are tearful, and rejoice with them when they are triumphant. Availability to the children has afforded us the luxury of seeing first-hand the progress that the children make daily. It also allows us to respond to any challenges they may face.

An issue of great concern that many parents in the United States of America have had, which has intensified in the last five years, has been the issue of safety. Children have been tormented and even murdered in public schools at the hands of students. Teachers have been stalked and also murdered by students. When children are studying at home, their risk of persecution is obviously significantly reduced. Knowing that our children are safe and are utilizing their time for real study and development is another reward that home-educating families experience. They do not have to spend those precious learning hours in paranoia, wondering what is going to happen next. They are able to relax and focus.

One of the greatest rewards that our family has experienced as home-educators and students is the bonding between family members. The children encourage one another when they are studying and when they are playing. They are sensitive and responsive to the hurt that a brother may be experiencing. When one boy is really focusing well and is completing his work successfully, the others always say, "Good job! You are doing well!" When one of them is struggling, the others say, "Would you like some help? We know you can do it! We'll help you if you need it! You're a good boy!" Hearing encouraging words transferred from one boy's mouth to the other boy's ears is one of the sweetest things that we as their parents can hear.

Something that Carmelo and I believe is also important for successful home education is allowing opportunities for our children to study a particular subject under the guidance of another instructor. It is our duty as parents and home educators to check out the background of the instructor. If the instructor meets our standards, our children may take a course under that instructor's leadership. We believe it is our job to raise our children in the way they should go. We teach the standard of living to them, which includes conduct, attitude, and absolutes. We teach them to measure everything against Biblical standards. We teach them how to learn. We help them learn their academics. And as part of a balanced, healthy life experience, we believe that it is beneficial to them to occasionally study under the instruction of another teacher. The reason for this belief is that in life, we know that they will have to answer to someone else beside ourselves. We know they will have to learn to work with other students. Therefore, to adequately prepare them for life, we believe that it can only be a refining and strengthening process to allow them to study with others.

The best examples that I can give to you are the courses they are presently taking. The two oldest children, ages four and six, are each taking a six week course. These two courses meet every Saturday morning for one and one-half hours.

They are both science courses that are designed for gifted children. The boys enjoy studying with the other students. They are learning to practice their classroom manners in another classroom, one that is neither their homeschool classroom nor their Sunday School classroom. They see the importance of remaining who they are regardless of where they are, and regardless of what is happening around them. When other children are rude to some of the classmates, or even to the teacher, our boys never join in on the pandemonium. They stand firmly on principles that are everlasting. Their sense of identity is so engrained in their minds and hearts that no evil penetrates them. They are truly grateful to God the creator who made them. He is their shield against all evil.

For those of you who do not believe that it is possible for you to homeschool your child, but would like to, please pray to God. Ask Him for direction. If it is His will, He will show the way to you. Perhaps the way could be learning with your child. Another possibility is studying regularly with another homeschooling family. If the obstacles are finances, perhaps you could work at home in the evenings, developing a project on your own to generate income. Maybe you could work outside the home, in the evenings, to provide the needed income. Another option is that your spouse could make adjustments to provide additional income. If it is the Lord's will, and you are quiet enough and patient enough to listen to His answer to your prayer, you will hear it. It is up to you to act upon His answer.

Homeschooling, or home-based education, has another benefit. When you and your family are studying a particular topic, you have the freedom of deciding when and where you will take your field trips to further understand your subject matter. When Carmelo had completed teaching the boys about the architectural designs of arches with diagrams and labels and discussion, he planned a field trip to the St. Louis Gateway Arch! The children looked at the arch and told us the names of the various parts and how they fit together. Then we went inside the arch and rode up to the top on a tram. We were 630 feet high in the air! When we arrived at our home, the boys asked us to get some art supplies for them. They made arches with labels reflecting what they had learned on their field trip! Experiencing a subject is a great way to solidify book knowledge.

Another example of homeschooling freedom and experiential learning is our study of various African and Asian animals. After we researched them at home, wrote about them, and made construction paper replicas of them, we went to the zoo with our cameras to see them! The children were able to properly identify the animals by name, continent of origin, climate, diet, approximate weight, height, and length, behavioral patterns, and uses for peculiar physical characteristics. They particularly enjoyed watching the Asian elephant lift straw with its trunk.

Home-based education is a blessing to a family who seeks God first. There are no unknown factors to the parents concerning their children. The children have such a strong identity that they do not seek negatively influential children as playmates to follow and copy. Rather, they change the other children's focus. Here is an example from our family. When our sons encounter children who are negative, they befriend them, but take the leadership role. This completely changes the climate from an aggressive, ugly one, into a friendly, happy one! The children who had a rebellious attitude suddenly have a reason to smile. They recognize that someone cares enough about them to want them to do well. Love is action. Love is a spiritual gift that we are able to give to one another.

If homeschooling is done in your home, led by the Holy Spirit, you will raise your child to be a strong, virtuous citizen of Heaven. And while he is on this Earth, he will be less likely to compromise the principles that you have diligently and lovingly taught him.

If you really want to home-educate your child, and the local laws are permissible to do so, choose a mission for your homeschool. When the purpose of your homeschool is clear, select a name for your homeschool that reflects your school's direction. In our homeschool, Samuel and Peter selected the name Esho Christian Academy. In Aramaic, Esho means "Jesus." When I said I thought Esho Christian seemed redundant, the boys said they knew that most people would not know what "Esho" means. Therefore, they wanted "Christian" in their school name also, so there would be no doubt about how they study and whom they worship. The selection of a homeschool name will certainly identify your family. It will also bless the soul of your child as well as the souls of you, his parents.

Homeschooling is very effective for the soul, spirit, and body of the child and all of his family members. When home-based education is done properly, time is taken to truly nurture all of these aspects of the child. They are all present for a reason. They are all important, contributing factors to his identity!

CHAPTER 7
HOUSEHOLD HABITS

In this chapter, we will discuss various habits that many households practice. There will be examples of habits that contribute to the betterment of the household, as well as examples of habits that contribute to the deterioration of the household.

We will begin with examples of habits that extract energy from the family unit, contributing to the deterioration of the household. The first habit that comes to mind is the habit of getting the day started without Bible reading and prayer. Bible reading and prayer are essentials in laying the foundation for the day. They are essential because they literally put God first. When God is put first, He blesses.

Another negative household habit is the mind-numbing habit of television viewing. The main point to remember is that those whom you are watching are not concerned with the well-being of your family. So much time is wasted in front of television, yet people complain about the lack of time to spend with family members, to do housework and hobbies, to enjoy social activities or to simply be quiet and still. Viewing the news in the evening when the little ones are asleep is acceptable, but not during their precious, few waking hours. Television viewing seems to be a means of escape and fantasy, even sensational thrills. None of these are conductive to holy living. They contribute to the oppression of the soul by constantly presenting material that is based in secular, godless beliefs. They contribute to the dulling of the mind by presenting falsehoods as facts. They contribute to the decay of the body, because viewers just sit and eat while watching television. All of these negative contributions wage war against the soul, spirit, and body. Therefore, they will bring neither temporary nor eternal reward. We are in the midst of the greatest battle for the souls and spirits of our children, ever.

My least favorite habit the many parents and grandparents have is the habit of bribery. There is nothing more insulting to the integrity of your child than to teach him to accept bribes. Rules, expectations, and consequences should always be made clear, but coercion should never be used. Do not use bribery to save yourself from embarrassment in front of others. Your child will view you as insincere. Bribery teaches your child that for the right price, he can be bought. For some temporary, flashy prize that will soon decay, his character has been traded. This certainly represses his soul, and dulls his mind.

Duplicity is another habit that can destroy a family. It teaches your child that public and private behaviors and attitudes can be different, depending on who is around you. It makes you unreliable to those who should be the most important to you. Being duplicitous makes the child either want to raise himself and avoid repeating your example, or it will cause him to behave the same way that you have been behaving. Thus the cycle of phoniness will continue, and a truly peaceful household will seem impossible.

There is another household habit that, without thought, passes from one generation to another. It is the habit of laziness. Laziness comes in many forms. Sometimes parents claim they are too tired to correct their children when the children are behaving inappropriately. Sometimes the parents claim to be too tired to monitor and correct their own inappropriate behavior. Sometimes parents exhibit laziness by relying on the past accomplishments of family members to excuse and overlook what they are not doing today in their own homes. This can apply to the spiritual life of a family, and it can also apply to heritage. Procrastination is a form of laziness that should not be allowed to develop.

Some parents have excused their own lackluster energy toward their family by saying, “Well, my father was a physician. My grandmother was a professor.” That is very nice and commendable for the father and grandmother. But what are the parents doing today in their own households? What are the standards by which they and their children are living? I am not making a reference to material wealth, or personal glory. I am making a reference to a standard of excellence that each household should have for its family members, to the glory of God, who created them.

Here is another example of laziness. The laziness in relying on one’s heritage to justify how he lives today is so insulting to those who have come before him. If parents are descendents of a heritage that has been strong and mighty and they identify themselves with that heritage, and they are not using that same vigor to keep their own households in order, they do not deserve to take credit for other people’s hard work and faith. The strength of any nation is maintained when the members of its citizens’ homes are united. When all these people are relying on God as their source of strength and unity, He blesses that nation. Every nation that has taken its eyes off the one, true God, and has begun to rely on its own agenda, has become weakened by its own arrogance. God blesses those who bless Him. He curses those who curse Him. He is a just God. He does not appreciate laziness. Laziness is ultimately arrogance. Laziness is saying, "Everything that needed to be done has been done for me. I'll take credit for the diligence of others, and complain when the results are not the ones that I desire. I have more important, self-indulgent things to do with my time." Faith and diligence are not inherited characteristics, as are hair color and height. They are personal choices that we make.

However, when we choose to allow God to lead our homes in the way they should go, our children's souls, spirits, and bodies are blessed. Their souls are blessed because they are at peace. Their spirits are delighted because God never deceives. Their bodies receive proper care and protection because they realize that the body is the temple of God. Their minds are strengthened because they meditate and think on that which is pure and holy. Faith in God and diligence to do

His work are completely productive and eternally rewarding.

Here are some highly productive habits that will provide relief for you and your family. Develop a daily schedule to which you are willing to adhere. Be sure that the schedule begins with Bible reading and prayer. Writing a schedule and following it tells your family and yourself that your household is important enough to put priorities that affect everyone down on paper. Once that is accomplished, live by your schedule daily, making sure to be flexible when a real emergency presents itself. However, when a schedule is designed and followed, emergencies become a rarity. You have taken charge of how time will be spent. An organized home brings peace of mind.

Another habit that will bring peace of mind is the habit of employing humor. Humor is a result of joyful hearts. When your children are growing up confidently and securely, you will see that they laugh and develop jokes that are totally harmless in nature, and provide extra personality to the day. Avoid jokes that belittle people, or indicate an attitude of cruelty toward animals. Remember that all living things are God's creation. Humor should be used properly for the pleasure of those around us.

The most important task the parents need to accomplish, after prayer, is to establish a family statement. Decide what you believe God is leading your family to do for Him. When a decision has been reached, write a statement. Here are some examples. “Our home represents integrity.” “We are here to nurture one another.” “As for me and my house, we will serve the Lord.

A special family craft project can be the making of family statement plaques. Children can make their own family statement plaques for their rooms. The whole family can contribute to one that can be placed in the most frequented room in the home. Establishing a family statement, and then paying attention to it each day, will definitely set the tone for how your days will be spent.

Establishing a family statement and then living by it will provide the entire family with a wonderful sense of security and identity. This is especially important to children, who can afford no loss in identity and security. When children are being raised in a stable and nurturing environment, the proof that they are satisfied will be displayed in everything they do and say. Their play and study behavior will exhibit confidence. Confidence manifests itself in many different ways. Sharing of attention and possessions, encouragement to other children, modesty, and honesty are some of those ways. A nurturing, dependable environment is such a great gift to give to your child, and you should give it every day!

Another great habit to form is the installation and timely recognition of family traditions that reflect the personality of the family. Here are some examples of our family traditions. Every Christmas and Easter we prepare a meal that includes the ingredient lamb. To us, lamb is the essential ingredient, because Jesus was called the Lamb of God. We also always include pita bread, because Jesus was also called the Bread of Life. Each year, the menu is different, but it does include these two ingredients. It is also always a meal of Middle Eastern origin, usually Assyrian or Jewish. The reason for this is because Jesus spoke Aramaic, the Assyrian language, and he was called the King of the Jews. The other criterion is that the meal must be festive, one that reflects the importance of such a blessed occasion as the birth of our Savior and His triumph over death!

On Christmas, my husband, Carmelo, reads from the Bible about Jesus. He begins with the Old Testament prophecies about His birth. He finishes with the New Testament descriptions of what actually took place. This reading is done at the dining room table, before we pray and eat.

Gifts are exchanged in the late afternoon. The gifts the children receive are those that can be used to worship Jesus. Some of those gifts have been instruments. On Jesus' birthday, and everyday, beautiful music can be played to honor Him. The best comment that we, their parents, have heard from them, is that they have already received the greatest gift of all, God's love, Jesus. They have also said that if they did not receive gifts from us, it would be fine, because Jesus is timeless and priceless. They are extremely appreciative of what they have, and like to focus on how they can bless God, since He has blessed them so much. One way they bless God is by making gifts for Jesus. They make things such as paintings that depict which gifts of their hearts and character they want to give to Him.

Another holiday that has the same menu-planning pattern is Easter. We spend the day rejoicing in our Risen Savior, and recognize the elements of rebirth and an entirely new life in Him.

Our family tradition, which we believe to be sound in content, is that we do not mix secular with sacred. That which is sacred should remain sacred, and undefiled. We do not believe in dressing down a holy holiday with the emptiness of secular celebrations. They are competing for attention, and are ultimately insulting to a Holy God. He who was blameless and who came to live among us to receive our sin upon Himself, and who died the most humiliating, cruel death for our wretched souls, deserves our full attention! No distractions are allowed!

Another tradition is that on patriotic holidays, the children receive a full week's worth of lessons pertaining to that holiday. We believe that it is important for the children to know what has transpired in this country in which they live, and in which they experience freedom. We encourage them to honor God when they think about political decisions. We encourage them to honor God when they interact with fellow Americans. We teach them to have respect for our American soldiers who sacrifice their lives for our freedom. We teach them to respect those in governing positions, and to live in accordance with the law. We teach them that living by the law of the land is an act of obedience to God. He commands us to honor the government under which we live.

Another household habit that we employ is the habit of celebrating each season. We study weather patterns, the effect of the weather on nature, foods that are available in each season, proper dress for each season, and games that can be played during each season. We also develop traditions for each celebration. One example is that in the spring, we have what we call our Springtime Celebration. We study the new animals, we study the new plants, and we talk about the cycle of life; springtime is the time of rejuvenation, of new life. Carmelo and I then make colored eggs and hide them either in the house, or outside. The children search for them. When they find them, they eat what they can. Afterward, we have an art project relating to springtime. One year, the children painted wooden eggs and birdhouses. Then they drew pictures on a large poster-board that represented what springtime meant to them. They received little stuffed rabbits, and they still cuddle up with them today! They did appreciate what they learned, made, and received. However, what they said that really reflects the hearts of all children is that we think enough of them to have taken the time to put something together in which the whole family can participate. An important point to make is that if we were not available on ordinary days, with no special holiday festivities taking place, these special celebrations would be meaningless to them. They would think that they are not anything special themselves, without another distraction at stake. When we are available for our children for the simple fact that they are given to us to receive our care and protection, extra events can actually be enjoyed.

A tradition that Carmelo started when we were first married was the tradition of his early morning (6:00 A.M.-7:00 A.M.) grocery shopping and feast preparation on Saturday mornings. Every Saturday, the meal consists of eggs, scrambled with fresh herbs, beef sausage links, freshly baked and toasted bagels, American, Colby or Swiss cheese, cream cheese, fruit jam, fresh fruit, and a glass of juice. The children and I always look forward to Saturdays. Throughout Saturday and Sunday, Carmelo prepares all meals. This tradition shows our sons how important we are to their father. This lesson is one of many that demonstrates commitment. The children are being taught by volunteered, cheerful action. Due to the contrast with our usual breakfasts that I prepare, Carmelo's input is strong. To have balance in any home, both parents should contribute something that reflects their personalities.

Another tradition about which Carmelo has been emphatic is the tradition of keeping Sunday holy. We do not go shopping on Sunday, we do not go to parties on Sunday, and we do work on Sunday. This tradition has been developed out of love and respect for our Holy God. It is an act of obedience. We cheerfully obey. Obedience provides freedom. Carmelo spends the entire afternoon teaching the children, using the Bible as his textbook. They review their sermon notes and Sunday School lessons. They expand upon them by looking up the passages in the Bible. They take notes in spiral notebooks that have been designated for Bible lessons. They research and discuss new vocabulary. The whole day is devoted to honoring God and to studying His Word.

We believe that in establishing traditions that reflect our family's personality, a great sense of belonging is obtained. Eliminating habits that detract from the focus of the family will greatly enhance your effectiveness as parents. Eliminating these negative habits will make your child recognize that he matters. The shape of his character is the priority. Creating productive habits for your child and for all family members nurtures the soul. They, your child and all family members, are focused on living for God. Creating productive habits for your child and all family members nurtures the spirit. Sights are lifted. A triumphant and joyous living experience is the norm. Creating productive habits for your child and for all family members nurtures the body. The immune system is strengthened when there is an established, positive routine. The body language is also strengthened, and it reflects confidence. Creating productive habits for your child and all family members, nurtures the mind. It (the mind) is able to think with clarity when there is a positive pattern of action in the home.

Another habit that we encourage in our home is the recognition of the value of our experiences. We encourage our children to have an attitude of gratitude. We teach them to seek the value in that which they encounter, whether the experiences are pleasant or unpleasant. Oftentimes, our most unpleasant experiences are our most intense and most meaningful teachers.

We teach them to have an attitude of gratitude toward each other. They are grateful to have brothers with whom they can play each day. They are grateful for the different elements of play that each child brings into the group situation. They are grateful for the humor that each brother brings into the play experience.

The two older children have expressed gratitude for our teaching of virtue, and correction of sin. The eldest boy says he is grateful to have parents who love him and his brothers enough to teach them the difference between right and wrong. He also thanks us for not allowing them to continue in their sin. Imagine a child thanking a parent for not letting him get his way!

Another area where the children are taught to have an attitude of gratitude is the area of possessions. They are grateful for their home, clothing, food, toys and school supplies. They are grateful for our car, in which we can all fit safely.

They are also grateful for people with whom we can interact. For some of those people, we are students. For others, we are teachers.

The children have an attitude of gratitude toward God, who has allowed them to have these experiences, people, and possessions. Ultimately, they are exceedingly grateful for Jesus, and God's plan of salvation and redemption.

A really great habit to help your child form is the habit of using good manners. Using good manners is a blessing to the child's soul. The child's soul is blessed when he uses good manners because he has internal satisfaction in knowing that he has done what is right and appreciated by his parents and by God. Children who do not use good manners have a burdened soul. They are defensive for reasons unknown to others, and show their rebellion in using crude manners. Poor manners are a symptom of a soul that is deprived of nourishment. When a child's best interests are a priority to his parents, his good manners will reflect the care he is receiving. His soul is at peace. The part of the soul that is his mind is blessed when he uses good manners because he has to think and remember the rules that he rules that he has been taught. Thinking keeps the mind active, and reduces mental laziness.

Here are some examples of teaching your

child to have and utilize good manners.

Teach him to say, “May I please use the computer, Dad?” “May I please be excused from the table, Mom?”

Another way to use good manners is by addressing people by their proper titles. We have taught our sons that they are to call any female between the ages of ten years and eighteen years Miss (Her First Name). Any female over the age of eighteen they are to call her Miss (Her Last Name), or Mrs. (Her Last Name). Regarding any male, the boys are to call him Mr. (His First Name), if he is between ten years and eighteen years. If he is older than eighteen years, they call him Mr. (His Last Name).

This next example applies mainly to male children. Another example of teaching your child to use good manners is to teach him to open doors for people, especially ladies. This should be followed by offering chairs to ladies, and to put the needs of ladies before his own. Whenever I am preparing to sit somewhere, Samuel and Peter both offer to pull my chair out for me. Whenever I am ready to pass through a doorway, they both want to open the door. These acts of kindness in their manners indicate to me that the very important lessons of respect and unselfishness are welcome in their hearts. Good manners are a by-product of a heart at peace, and of teaching that is consistent and loving. Teaching young boys how to be gentlemen trains them for how they will be expected to behave when they are men.

There is another habit that is a must for any family. It is the habit of insisting that the best of everything that each family member has to contribute must be focused on home and church first. It matters not how impressive we are to others. If we do not treat our family members well, and if we do not treat our Christian family well, we should be ashamed. God has placed specific people in our lives for a purpose. They should never, nor should He, ever receive our discards. Teach your children to speak respectfully to family members, and about family members. Teach them to dress nicely when they are home. Teach them to employ the best of what they have to offer to their home family members and to those in the Christian family. God is glorified when His children seek to obey Him. He is glorified when we put Him and His commandments first. Children are instructed to obey their parents. Parents are instructed to not provoke their children to anger. If we practice what we say we believe at home, and bring it to church, then we are reliable witnesses to the rest of the world regarding our sincerity as believers.

As a part of being our best at home, we must encourage our children and spouse by making a habit of hospitality. We should be hospitable to one another in the family first. We should then invite those we love to join us at our tables. Hospitality teaches children to not be self-absorbed, but to serve others. In our home, we always eat our meals together. We encourage one another by talking about our day. We discuss what we learned from the experiences that day. We answer questions that arise. We assist each other with the meal. After we have prayed, Carmelo always waits until I have begun to eat. He then nods very discretely to the boys, allowing them to begin. He always starts his meal last. He is teaching the children respect for me, and he is expressing respect for them, in waiting until we are all satisfied before he begins. He is also using hospitality, because is playing the role of the servant. As Jesus Christ came to seek and save, He also served the needs of others. He washed the feet of His disciples, and He provided food and drink for them. So we should also teach our children hospitality. It is a much greater blessing to serve. It is a blessing that nurtures the spirit and mind. The spirit is nurtured because it is at peace in knowing that our behavior is pleasing to our Holy God. The mind is nurtured because it has to remember rules of manners and of serving.

Another positive habit that will surely bless not only your child, but also all family members and friends, is the habit of conflict resolution. Throughout the day, as exasperating situations arise, discourage fighting between the children that employ ugly words and physical harm. Encourage them to look one another in the eyes, and talk to one another in calm voices. Let them know they are entitled to be straightforward in their speech, but they are never to be hurtful by word or deed. Whenever one of the sons somehow hurts another one, the offending child looks his brother whom he hurt in the eyes. He states what he did, then apologizes for his behavior. The boy who was hurt looks in his brother's eyes and forgives him. They follow this apology and forgiveness with hugs. Jesus taught us to be honest, courageous, and forgiving. Following Jesus' example is a habit that can only bless a household.

The final habit that I will address is the habit of questioning our own thoughts and actions. When you are thinking about doing something, or are actually doing it, ask a question of yourself. Say something like, "What is the purpose of this? What will it accomplish? Will it be pleasing to God? Will this shame my family? Is this contributing to, or detracting from, our family statement?" Do not act impulsively. When you have your answers, make adjustments as needed. Live according to God's word. No man has ever been wiser than God. No man ever will be wiser than God.

CHAPTER 8
GRANDPARENTS ARE SPECIAL

Grandparents are special! After all, they brought your spouse and you to the place you are now! Grandparents are extra special to children, especially when they get down on the floor and play with them, or tell a funny story to them.

Here are some wonderful ways that grandparents can use to cultivate beautiful and lasting relationships with their grandchildren.

The first way, and most important way, that grandparents and grandchildren can grow together is the sharing of their faith. If the beliefs are not the same, then real intimacy and identity will not result. If the grandparents and the grandchildren do have the same faith, then identifying with other family members will broaden. The grandchildren's points of reference will broaden. The rest of the ways that grandparents can use to cultivate great relationships with their grandchildren depend on shared faith. If they have the same beliefs, then all of their experiences together will be genuine and treasured.

The second way that grandparents can cultivate great relationships with their grandchildren is through the passing on of heritage. Every heritage has a set of traditions and stories that are based on a belief system.

Everything from prayer style, food choices and meal preparation, holidays, music, dance, and personal grooming and dress, to history, geography and language are all based on the spiritual beliefs of that culture. Connecting with one's heritage is not only a great way to ensure identity, it is also a great way to honor and appreciate those who have preceded you.

The third way that grandparents can cultivate meaningful relationships with their grandchildren is by celebrating holidays together. Religious holidays, birthdays, cultural New Year festivities and Grandparents' Day are the most important holidays. Celebrating these holidays together, and establishing a traditional, multi-generational family style of celebration is a fantastic way to create some beautiful moments and memories. Every year, we plan something for Grandparents' Day to show our love, respect and appreciation for our children's grandparents.

Another way that grandparents and grandchildren can bond with each other is by spending time studying together. Here are some examples of what our children and their grandparents have done together with regard to intellectual enrichment. Once a week, their grandparents came to our home. Grandma brought a new book to give to the children. Grandpa came with engineering skills. While Grandma listened to Peter read the new book she brought with her, Grandpa taught Samuel how to design a certain type of aircraft. Then Grandma read the story that she had brought to Peter. When Samuel and Grandpa were finished with their design lesson, Samuel and Peter traded places. Samuel read the new story to Grandma, while Peter received a lesson in aircraft design. During that time, Emmanuel watched his Grandpa draw, and he attempted to do the same. I took photographs of these sessions, which were placed in the boys' personal photograph albums. Copies of these photographs were given to their grandparents.

The role of grandparents is very important in the lives of their grandchildren. They should never disrespect the rules that the parents set for their children. When grandparents overstep the boundaries, the grandchildren see their grandparents in an uncomfortably negative light. They begin to distrust their grandparents, because they see them willingly discounting the value of the training and standards their parents have set for them. Grandparents are very important, precious people. They should always remember how sensitive their children and grandchildren are to their thoughts and behavior.

We are fortunate to enjoy open communication with our children's grandparents. If any concerns arise, both parties feel at ease to discuss them. Due to our understanding of each other and our respect for one another, these occasions rarely occur. To the grandparents of our sons, Castrenze and Rosa Turdo, God Bless You.

Productive, effective relationships between grandchildren and grandparents highly affect the souls of not only the grandchildren, but the souls of their parents and grandparents as well. All of these family members are able to relax and enjoy one another's company when they have the same goal.

CHAPTER 9
RECIPES THAT REFLECT HERITAGE

In this last chapter, I will choose to write two recipes, each representing the cultural heritage that is in our home. It is important to remember that each family has its own style of interpreting recipes. These recipes reflect our style,

We enjoy mealtime. It is a time when all five of us are sitting together, relaxing and enjoying one another's company. The most important point that we make to our children is that not only are we passing on to them our ethnic heritage, we are primarily passing on to them a Christian heritage. Our sole purpose in this season of life is to raise these three boys to become godly, virtuous men of character, strength and humility. I hope that you enjoy these recipes from our kitchen, and will receive them into yours. God bless you and your family.

Sincerely,

Susie Turdo

JADGICK TREEDA--ASSYRIAN RECIPE

Pour one-half gallon of whole milk into a 3-quart saucepan. With the lid off, set the stovetop burner on low heat. Allow milk to reach its boil slowly to avoid burning the milk on the bottom of the pan. With a wooden spoon slowly stir the milk, making sure to touch the bottom of the saucepan. Allow the milk to boil slowly, on low heat, until you see a skin form on top of the milk. Shut off the heat and very carefully pour the boiled milk into a clean, large glass storage container. Do not put the lid on the container. After a few minutes, dip your pinky finger into the milk. If it is hot, but does not burn your skin, place 4-5 tablespoons of whole milk yogurt into the container with the milk. Slowly and thoroughly stir the milk and the yogurt together. Place the lid on the container, sealing out the air. Wrap the container in several heavy towels or blankets. Place it out of the way in a room temperature spot that is free of breezes. In about 24 hours, check your mixture for thickness. It should be almost as thick as yogurt is when it is by itself. Stir the mixture thoroughly. This mixture is called Mesta. If it has thickened properly, refrigerate it without the towels or blankets. When the Mesta has chilled, it is edible by itself or mixed into hot cereal or other boiled or steamed grain. It is delicious and highly nutritious. To make Jadgick Treeda from Mesta, chop one small or medium size red or white onion. These pieces should be no wider or taller than one-half centimeter. Chop some scallions into one-half centimeter long pieces. Chop several cloves of fresh garlic into little chunks and slivers. Chop fresh dill into one-half centimeter long pieces. Sprinkling dried dill is also acceptable. Find a firm, crisp cucumber. Peel it in an alternating pattern and chop it into centimeter size chunks. Be sure to wash and dry the onions, garlic, dill, and cucumber before you use them. Stir these ingredients thoroughly into the Mesta. You may eat the jadgick treeda this way, or you may sprinkle a pinch of salt, and even add a splash of white vinegar or fresh lemon juice if you so desire. I personally think it is a great dish, even without adding salt and vinegar or lemon juice. Jadgick treeda is a very cool, refreshing side dish. It is also highly nutritious and is effective in battling infections such as those associated with colds. Each batch of jadgick treeda will remain fresh in the refrigerator for two weeks.

I hope you enjoy one of our family favorites!

TOMATO SAUCE—ITALIAN RECIPE

Wash and slice dozens of Roma tomatoes. Heirloom tomatoes of multiple colors had juiciness to the body of the sauce, in addition to a pleasing appearance. Place them in an 8-quart stockpot. Add sun-dried tomatoes and 24 ounces of regular tomato paste. Avoid the ones with added flavors. Contadina is the best brand for tomato paste. With the lid on the pot, turn the stovetop burner onto medium heat. Every two to three minutes stir the tomato contents, making sure that the spoon is touching the bottom of the pot. The spoon should be wooden. Wash and slice a large white or yellow onion. The pieces should be one centimeter in height and length. Stir them into the tomato mixture. Wash and cut three portabella mushrooms into 1 centimeter-cubed chunks. Use a medium or large sauté pan, 10"-12" in diameter. Pour approximately 2 tablespoons of extra virgin olive oil into the pan. Set the stovetop burner to medium heat. When the oil is hot, put portabella chunks into oiled pan. Stir regularly. Sprinkle a pinch of coarse kosher salt on top of the mushroom chunks. When these chunks have been well cooked, pour them into the 8-quart stockpot.

Reduce the heat to a low setting. Wash and slice three zucchini squash into 1 centimeter cubed chunks. Repeat with the zucchini what you did with the portabella mushrooms. Peel and cut into thick chunks one head of garlic. Stir it into the pot with all the other ingredients. For added sumptuous flavor, add browned ground beef or veal to the sauce. Stir thoroughly, keeping stovetop burner setting on low heat. Wash and slice into 1 centimeter long pieces fresh scallions, parsley, and cilantro. Add a handful of fresh or dried green sweet basil and oregano for a truly delicious and nutritious tomato sauce. Stir the dried herbs into the sauce first before stirring in the fresh ones. Serve the tomato sauce over your favorite pasta. Any leftover sauce may be stored in the freezer for a few months.

ABOUT THE AUTHOR

Susie Turdo was born in St. Paul, Minnesota. She lived in Minnesota for nearly five and one-half years. In her second home located in Duluth, Minnesota, she prayed and received the Lord Jesus Christ as her personal Savior at the age of four years. From that point she relied upon the strength of her Creator to overcome many adversities. Her family relocated to St. Louis, Missouri where she was raised. She studied Pre-Med, French, and English at the University of Missouri-St. Louis. There she met her future husband Carmelo Turdo. She lived and worked in Chicago, Illinois for several months, before returning to St. Louis to be married. In the first four and a half years of marriage, three fabulous sons were born to Carmelo and Susie!

Her heart's desire has always been to live near her relatives. Some of her best childhood memories are of her grandparents, Samuel and Martha Joseph. Their prayer, humor and delicious Mesta have been a tremendous source of inspiration. Some other great memories are of cousins, particularly Paul and Mary David. They taught her gentleness, hospitality, and respect for each spouse. She is extremely grateful to her relatives, of Assyrian heritage, who have sacrificed their lives in order to provide their descendents with a place to live that is free from daily torment. She is grateful to the Assyrian people for not forgetting who they are, and for allowing God, who has kept them alive since Genesis, to be their strength.

ABOUT THE ILLUSTRATOR

Carmelo Turdo was born and raised in Florissant, MO. He received the Lord Jesus Christ as his personal Savior at the age of thirteen years. He attended Christian Brothers College High School in St. Louis and studied Political Science and English at Norwich University, the Military College of Vermont. He later received a Masters Degree at the University of Missouri-St. Louis. There he met his future wife, Susie. In the first four and one-half years of marriage, three fabulous sons were born to Carmelo and Susie!

Carmelo's interests include aviation, playing percussion instruments, writing, and home education. He will soon combine all of these interests by producing educational books for children, featuring the history of aviation and percussion instruments. He is grateful for the support he has received from his parents and his family, and most of all strives to receive and fulfill the will of God in his life.

THE FUTURE

Susie and Carmelo are presently writing academic and Bible storybooks for young children, and for the young at heart. They are thoroughly appreciating and enjoying this precious season of life, the time of nurturing and raising their sons to be men of God.

The Turdo Family thanks you for the purchase of this book. May God use it to bless you and your family. Shlama (Peace).

www.ingramcontent.com/pod-product-compliance
Ingram Content Group UK Ltd.
Pitfield, Milton Keynes, MK11 3LW, UK
UKHW020127250726
13967UKWH00002B/526

9 781304 669254